EXPECT A MOVE OF GOD IN YOUR LIFE . . . SUDDENLY!

D0664382

Unless otherwise indicated, all Scripture quotations are taken from *The Amplified Bible* (AMP). *Old Testament* copyright © 1965, 1987 by The Zondervan Corporation, Grand Rapids, Michigan. *New Testament* copyright © 1954, 1958, 1987 by The Lockman Foundation. Used by permission.

Scripture quotations marked (KJV) are taken from the *King James Version* of the Bible.

FaithWords
Hachette Book Group USA
237 Park Avenue
New York, NY 10169

Visit our Web site at www.faithwords.com.

Printed in the United States of America

First Warner Faith Edition: February 2003

10 9 8 7

The FaithWords name and logo are trademarks of Hachette Book Group USA.

ISBN 978-0-446-69195-6 (Special Sales Edition)

EXPECT A MOVE OF GOD IN YOUR LIFE . . . SUDDENLY!

JOYCE MEYER

NEW YORK   BOSTON   NASHVILLE

EXPECT A MOVE OF GOD
IN YOUR LIFE . . . SUDDENLY!

There is a word that I want to deposit in you through God's Word that you can hang onto for the rest of your life, and I hope you never forget it. It is the word *suddenly*!

Sometimes when you have lived with something in your life a long, long time, you get to the point that you can limp along with it and go on about your business at the same time. But God heard those prayers that you prayed about the situation, and He remembers them. Then *suddenly* He can move in your life and deliver you in a way that will just amaze you. I believe we need to *expect* God to move *suddenly*!

God Moves Suddenly!

My daughter, Sandra, had some longstanding problems like you, like me, like everybody. They weren't just one or two week problems. They were problems that she had struggled with nearly all of her life. And then one night at one of my meetings *God moved suddenly and delivered her.*

I believe we were in Tulsa, Oklahoma at the time, and she was working in the ministry of helps as she always does at my meetings. But this night was different, and I knew God was going to do something special for her. Normally, she doesn't even get to come in for the worship, but on this night, she was drawn in by the worship.

When she saw me, she knew something was going on because I kept looking at her. Then, just

all of a sudden, I knew I was supposed to pray for her, so I called her up front and told her, "This is the end of it. You're getting a release from some of those longstanding problems you've had."

When I laid my hands on her, I could tangibly sense the anointing of God and feel virtue go out from me. When it did, she fell out in the Spirit and just laid there for a while because God was doing something in her. When she got up, she was shaking all over. She didn't know at the time what God was going to do. She didn't have it all figured out, but she knew that she would see the results of it in time.

After about a month, she began to change in the areas that she had been believing God for. She had even written a few of them down as New Year's resolutions. She didn't figure out how she was going to change herself—God just touched her, and it happened.

Now she has a lot more peace. In high-pressured situations, she doesn't lose her temper anymore or start crying. She is also able to trust God more so that when she has more to do than she has time for, she is able to rely on Him to work it out and to give her His peace in the midst of the *situation*.

She also has more confidence to make decisions than she used to. She is no longer afraid that every decision she makes is going to be imperfect or worries about getting corrected for making a wrong decision.

Another thing she was having difficulty with was accepting herself just the way God made her. She kept comparing her looks with other women's and would say to herself things like, "Oh, she is pretty. I wish I had hair like hers or a complexion like hers." Now she doesn't do that anymore either. Those thoughts have simply disappeared.

Sometimes she even teases with her husband and says, "She has nice hair, but I don't want to look like her. I like the way I am." She doesn't worry anymore so much about what others think of her. She isn't perfect, but she knows God is working with her and is in the process of changing her.

When she does slip back into the way she used to think and feel, she doesn't say, "Well, that's it! I thought God had changed me. Now I'm making the same mistakes again. Just forget it. I haven't really changed."

As long as we are alive on this earth, we aren't going to be perfect, but God is bringing us along the way, and He just keeps changing us and changing us and changing us.

You Aren't Hopeless

Of course, the devil wants you to feel stuck in your situation and convince you that it is hopeless. He wants you to have those little thoughts in the back of your mind that say, "You aren't ever going to be any different. It isn't ever going to change. You'll never change. Your marriage will never change. Your financial situation will never change." That is what the devil says.

Regardless of what you know, he will say, "You'll be dumb all your life. You're never going to get your act together. Everyone in the room but you is getting touched by God. You're the only one who God isn't doing anything for." Do you know that these thoughts are really attacks from the devil? But remember, the devil is a liar (John 8:44), so every thought he gives you will be a lie.

You need to learn what God says about you in His Word so that you will recognize any thought not in line with what God says as coming from the devil. If you are very smart at all, you aren't going to believe it. Things don't have to get as complicated as we sometimes make them.

You can change *suddenly*! Your situation can change *suddenly*! And that is great news. I want to get up every day with the expectancy, "God may do something suddenly today!" Things can and do change *suddenly*.

All You Have to Do Is Wait

Before God moves suddenly, though, you must wait. In Acts 1:4, it says, **And while being in their company and eating at the table with them, He commanded them.** In other words, this was not just a nice suggestion. He commanded them. He commanded them not to leave Jerusalem but to *wait* for what the Father had promised.

Waiting the way God means to wait is something we probably really don't know very much

7

about. Waiting on God isn't some passive apathetic mode you get into when you get depressed and just sit back and do nothing. It means you do only what God tells you to do, what God anoints you to do and what God gives you permission to do. Then you don't do anything else until God tells you to do something else.

If He tells you to do only one thing this year concerning your circumstance, then He doesn't tell you to do another thing for six months, you won't do something He didn't tell you to do for anything. You know that what is born of flesh is flesh, and the flesh profits nothing. (John 3:6, 6:63.)

It is really just a spiritual law that comes straight from the Bible. If you want the promises of God, then you are going to get them by waiting. In Acts 1:4, the promise of the Father they are waiting for is the pouring out of the Holy Spirit.

Personally, I think waiting involves two realms—the outer and the inner. In the outer realm, it means not going out in the flesh and physically creating a lot of activity to try and make something happen. You probably understand what I mean here quite well because I think we have all been there at one time or another. We were out there trying to make it happen, but God wasn't in it.

But waiting is more than not stepping out in the flesh, it is an inner waiting, and it goes on in your soul, in your inner man. When you have an inner waiting, your mind is at peace, and your will is at peace, and everything in you has come to a place of waiting on God.

You Can't Do It in Your Flesh

Before you can get to that point, you have to completely run out of trying to do it yourself.

Until you are thoroughly convinced you can't do yourself whatever it is you are trying to do, you can't really wait on God. You have to get to the point of not only knowing you can't do it, but you also have to know that if you touch it, you will foul it up! You cannot trust yourself to solve your problems.

I always get amused when I think about what happened to Abraham when God came to cut the covenant with him in Genesis 15. They cut the animal down the middle and spread the pieces out, then God knocked Abraham out cold and put him into a deep, deep sleep. God didn't even let Abraham get involved in confirming the covenant.

Genesis 15:17 says that a flaming torch passed between those pieces. That flaming torch was the Lord binding Himself to fulfill His promise in the covenant. Abraham didn't have anything to do with it! Abraham's only part was to believe.

Many people desperately need to get hold of this. Abraham's only part was *to believe*! He understood what it meant to make a covenant. He knew all about sacrificing the animal and walking in between the pieces. He knew all about that because it was something they did on a regular basis.

So I suppose that Abraham was pretty excited when he saw what God was going to do. But then God said, "Good night, Abraham. You can't have anything to do with this because you will foul it up. You will just mess it up, so go to sleep. Tomorrow you will know what has happened."

The disciples in the book of Acts weren't any different than Abraham because God commanded them to wait for the promise of the Holy

Spirit. He said, "Don't you try to go out and do any mighty acts until you receive the promise of the Holy Spirit that is going to be sent."

Waiting Releases the Anointing

Sometimes we assume that just because we are baptized in the Holy Spirit, *we* have the power to do something we see that needs to be done, and we think we should do it. We do have that power available to us, but what we think should be done may not be what God wants at that time. Instead, we need to learn how to wait on God in each instance for the power of the Holy Spirit. When we wait on God, His anointing is released because we honor Him by waiting and refusing to move without Him.

It is also good to wait in prayer. Many times we go into prayer and start talking ninety miles a minute without even thinking about what God may be saying. Instead, we need to go into prayer and humble ourselves by saying, "God, I don't know what to say. I don't have anything to say that is going to make any sense. If You don't anoint this, it isn't going to get through, so I'm just going to wait here on You."

When you just wait on God, the anointing will be released! You will begin to sense it coming upon you as you wait, and it will enable you to do what you ought to do and want to do. So often though, even when we are doing what we ought to do and want to do, even when we are doing the right thing, if we haven't honored God by waiting on Him, we are still running in the flesh. It won't work.

Sometimes we may find ourselves in a situation where someone needs to be confronted and something needs to be said. But instead of waiting on God, we just run into it with our mouth wide open, blabbing away. We haven't waited on

God. We haven't waited for His timing, and we just make a big mess.

Then we come running back to God saying, "Well, God, I thought it was the right thing to do, and I thought You put it on my heart! I don't understand why everybody is mad and upset. Why didn't it work?" It didn't work because we didn't wait on God!

Sometimes we just get full of ourselves! We think, "I know what I'll do . . ." then the power of the flesh comes zinging through and fills us full of so many great, nifty, little cutesy ideas! And we wonder why we fail every time we turn around. The idea might have been good, but it won't work if we don't wait on God.

Waiting Brings Life

Recently we were getting ready to host a *Life In The Word* meeting in a large hotel ballroom and weren't able to get into the room until ten after four when usually we have all day to prepare the room. The meeting was to start at seven, and you should have seen the place! People were buzzing in and out. The equipment was being unloaded and set up, the flowers had arrived and were being arranged, and we were there praying.

While we were praying, God gave me this vision of when He created Adam. The frame of Adam was all together, but until God breathed into him the breath of life, Adam was just a lifeless blob. Now, read this carefully and remember it: No matter what you or I come up with, no matter how good an idea it is, no matter how much it ought to work and no matter how many people have done it before and it worked for them, if we don't wait on God to breathe the breath of life into it, it isn't going to get up on its feet and live!

Sometimes we are just so busy doing so many things we completely miss what God wants us to do. We would do well to do a whole lot less *doing* and a whole lot more *waiting*.

Waiting Brings Power

In Acts 1:8, Jesus told his disciples:

> But you shall receive power (ability, efficiency, and might) when the Holy Spirit has come upon you, and you shall be My witnesses in Jerusalem and all Jude and Samurai and to the ends (the very bounds) of the earth.

In other words, he was saying, "Wait and you'll receive the *power* that comes from on high when the Holy Spirit comes upon you. Don't you try to go out and do any mighty works until you've received that *power.*" And they knew that if they didn't wait that they weren't going to have power. So His disciples waited, and they did what He told them to do.

Now this isn't just something His disciples should do. It is a principle that applies to us today. It is a spiritual law. Once again, I'm not saying, "Don't step out in faith"; I'm saying to "actively" wait for the promises of God by listening for what He is telling you to do instead of running out there and doing something in the flesh. You must *wait* for the promises of God.

Ishmael was the child of Abraham and Sarah's fleshly works. Ishmael was a man of war. Genesis 16:11,12 (KJV) says of Ishmael: **the angel of the Lord said . . . he will be a wild man; his hand will be against every man, and every man's hand against him. . . .** But the child of promise was Isaac which means "laughter."[1]

You can get an Ishmael any time you want, but if you want an Isaac, you will have to wait because you have to wait for the promises of God. And don't forget that when you get impatient waiting and have an Ishmael instead, you may spend the rest of your life changing his diapers! So think twice before you decide to rush ahead of God's timing. If you wait, you will receive what God has promised with power.

How Long Should You Wait?

There is another word in the Amplified version of Acts 1:13 that I also want to share with you. It reads as follows:

> And when they had entered [the city], they mounted [the stairs] to the upper room where they were [indefinitely] staying—Peter and John and James

and Andrew; Philip and Thomas,
Bartholomew and Matthew; James son
of Alphaeus and Simon the Zealot,
and Judas [son] of James.

All of these with their minds in
full agreement devoted themselves
steadfastly to prayer, [waiting
together] with the women and Mary
the mother of Jesus, and with His
brothers.

The key word here is *indefinitely.* They went
into the upper room with a mindset that said,
"We aren't coming out of here until God shows
up." They didn't go in there to wait ten minutes.
They didn't go in there to wait two days. They
didn't go in there to wait three months. No, they
went in there saying, "We can't do anything until
God shows up. So, God, I'm not moving until
You get here. I'm staying here *indefinitely*!"

When I read that, I thought, "Right there is our problem." Because we have so much energy and zeal in our flesh that even if we ever get around to waiting or trying to understand what it is, we only do it for short periods of time and then the energy of our flesh takes over *again*.

If God doesn't do something when we want Him to do it or as quick as we want Him to do it, then our bright ideas overtake us again, and we get right back in the flesh. We are constantly covering the same ground over and over again. We get a little ground, then we lose it. We gain a little ground, then we lose it.

The mindset we need to get is this: "Okay, God, I've come to the end of myself. I've tried this, and I've tried that. I've tried everything I can possibly think of for all these years. Now it has become obvious that I can't pull this off by myself. God, I need You. Only You can do it. So I'm waiting on You."

Whatever *it* is that you need God to do, you will have to wait. If it is seeing one of your children change, I guarantee you that you can't do it in your own strength, on your own time schedule. If it is changing the person you are married to, I can promise you that you can't do it either. If it is changing yourself, you can't do it. If it is getting a circumstance to change, you can't make it change. If it has something to do with your business or your finances, you can't change it. Whatever *it* is doesn't matter because you can't make it change!

But you can wait on God, and He can do it! You might have to wait more than five minutes or ten minutes or two weeks. You might have to wait *indefinitely.* But while you wait, you can have an attitude of knowing that God is going to do it.

Change Comes in His Presence

When I think back on my own emotional healing and all the messy problems I had from what I

21

went through in my past and the abuse and the hurts and how messed up I was inside, I thank God that He found a way to heal me. God knows I tried. I tried this person's formula and that person's formula. I tried so many different things.

I finally got to the point where I knew I had to have a set-apart time with God. I had to have a place that I went on a regular basis where I could just sit with God. Sometimes all I did was cry. Sometimes I would read the Word. Whenever I went, I went as a little child saying, "God, I can't help myself, and if You don't change me, I will stay this way until the trumpet blows and You return to get us."

Eventually I got to the point where I didn't really have any pressure on me because I knew He loved me. I knew I didn't have to change to please God because He loved me just the way I was. When I did change, it wasn't because I *had* to change to please God; it was because I *wanted* to change. It was because I wanted to be every-thing He wanted me to be. He was the only One Who could have helped me at the point where I was. He was the only One Who could have done it!

But I didn't get to that place of trust, that place of waiting, overnight. It took me years and years of suffering because of trying to do it my way and failing, or of trying to do it someone else's way and failing. It took me that long to come to the point of finally saying, "God, You have to change me. I can't do it."

When I finally began to trust Him to change me, I would just go and sit in His Presence. I can't tell you what He did, but I do know that He moved in my life, and He healed me. If you were to ask me how I received my healing, I would tell you that ninety-eight percent of it came simply while I was waiting in the presence of God in addition to regularly studying His Word.

You Have to Walk by Faith

When my daughter, Sandra, was prayed for and began to shake under the power of God, she didn't feel any different when she went home that night. She didn't see any immediate changes in her life the next day. But she believed that God had done something, that He was doing something and that she would see the fruit of it after a period of time. That is what I call faith!

After six weeks had passed, she looked back and saw that she had changed. Not only could she tell she had changed, others noticed she had changed. Now she is so much more peaceful. Things aren't bothering her the way they used to. Before, she wouldn't make even the simplest decision because she was so petrified of being wrong, but now she is gaining confidence in her ability to make a decision and, as a result, is taking on much more responsibility. And, she is doing such an excellent job with it!

Just a few months before, it wasn't that way in her life. She had been living with this mess for a long period of time and was trusting God to move in her life. She kept saying, "God, I can't do it, but You can. I can't do it, but You can." Then one night God moved. He touched her, and she received whatever He had for her and began to walk in it by faith.

What Are You Going to Do?

Sometimes you just need to stop trying to figure out what you ought to be doing in a situation and spend more time trying to stay away from doing anything unless you are *absolutely* positive it is something that God is giving you to do.

Of course, when the pressure is on, one of the records you will hear playing over and over in your head is, "Well, what are you going to do? You have to do something. What are you going to do? You can't just stand there and look stupid. What are you going to do?"

Even your most well-meaning friends will come over and say, "Hey, I heard about your problem. Well, what are you going to do?" All you have to say is, "I'm going to wait on God. That is what I'm going to do." Of course, they will ask, "Well, how long are you going to do that?" Then all you have to say is, "Indefinitely!"

That is the key word—*indefinitely*. You have to come to the point where you are willing to wait indefinitely and say, "God, if You don't do something, You will find me in this same attitude when the trumpet blows because I'm staying out of works of the flesh. I'm staying out of trying to solve this without hearing what You want me to do." Do you know why? Because works do nothing but make you miserable.

Why the Ten Day Wait?

That is what the disciples in Acts 2:1 did: they waited indefinitely for the promise of the Holy Spirit to come. Ten days came, and ten days went. But why did they have to wait for ten days? Andrew Murray in his book, *The Promise of the Spirit,* offers an interesting insight:

> Perhaps our faith may be tested by a
> prolonged wait, or by difficulties, but
> let us believe that God will satisfy our
> desire for His Spirit. I cannot think of
> anything which I find more wonderful
> and instructive, than the ten days of
> praying and waiting, which preceded
> the outpouring of the Holy Spirit at

Pentecost. It is a mystery. And I cannot understand it.

Jesus had died upon earth and had conquered sin. He had been raised from the dead, lifted up to the Father's Throne and glorified. He had received the Holy Spirit from the Father, so that He could give Him to the believers, and yet, despite all of this, there were ten days of waiting in Heaven.

God was ready, Christ was ready, the Holy Spirit was ready, the Trinity was ready, and yet, for ten days the Spirit could not come. Why? Because there had not yet been enough prayer.[2]

And I would add here, "And there had not yet been enough waiting." Jesus had spent three whole years preparing those disciples, everything

28

was ready in heaven, and yet those ten days were still needed. It isn't just praying that moves God. It is *waiting* and *praying* that moves God. You don't have to pray twenty-four hours continuously around the clock, but you do need to pray. They waited in that upper room, and they *prayed* earnestly.

Wait Patiently

I believe there is probably no greater evidence of faith than patient waiting. Our confession of faith may be good evidence. There may be all kinds of evidences. But there is no greater evidence of our faith than patient waiting on God in the midst of circumstances that scream at you saying, "You aren't going to get it!"

The Scriptures say that we are not only to wait, but we are to wait patiently. What does it mean to wait patiently? It is how we act *while* we are waiting. It doesn't mean we just put up with something. And it doesn't mean we have three fits every ten minutes while we are saying, "I'm waiting patiently on God."

No, that is waiting *im*patiently on God. We're still full of ourselves, still frustrated, still full of anxiety. We're still trying to make something happen in the flesh.

When we move into really waiting patiently, we're happy. We aren't frustrated. We have a sweet peace and a joy. We say to ourselves, "God, if You don't do this, it isn't going to get done. And there isn't any point in me making myself miserable from now until it happens because I've decided I'm waiting indefinitely, and I don't know if that means five minutes or five years."

The Church needs to get to the point where they stop making themselves miserable trying to make happen what only God can do.

That is what I call taking on a false sense of responsibility. Through the years, I have found that people operate in one of two realms—either they are taking no responsibility and won't do anything because they are lazy or they are messing around in God's business, trying to do what only God can do. I believe that the word of the Lord to the Church is, "Will you get your hands off of My business and let Me do what only I can do?"

You can put a frozen charismatic grin on your face, but that doesn't mean your soul is patiently waiting on God. It isn't what is on the outside I'm talking about; it is what is on the inside. You are patiently waiting on God when everything in you has come to a place of peace, and you are to the point of saying, "Well, God, if You don't do it, it isn't going to get done. And if You aren't going to do it or it isn't the right time, why should I fight it? This is Your deal, God, not mine. It is up to You! In the meantime, the Bible tells me I should go ahead and enjoy life, so that is exactly what I'm going to do. I'm going to enjoy life, and I'm going to wait for God to bring it to pass.

Wait Expectantly

What does it mean to wait? Well, it isn't just sitting down and being passive. It is an attitude of the heart that expects. To wait means to expect, to look for, to look for with a view to being shown favor. It carries the idea of waiting with patience and confident expectancy. In other words, you are expecting God to *suddenly* show up at any minute and change the whole mess in an instant!

Isn't it interesting that Andrew Murray says, "Those ten days of waiting were a mystery because everything was ready in heaven. God was ready! Jesus was ready! The Holy Spirit was ready!" Do you know how long the Holy Spirit had wanted to come? He had been waiting since the beginning of time! Now that is a lot of waiting. Can you imagine what it must have been like?

Now everything was in place. The time had come. The people were all assembled, and they were waiting. But it wasn't enough to wait five minutes. It wasn't enough to wait a half a day. One whole day went by, and still it wasn't time. Another day went by, and they were still waiting. Maybe by this time, they were getting tired of being in that room! Maybe some began to wonder if He was really going to come. But regardless of what they thought or felt, they continued to wait and to do what God had told them to do.

Then in Acts 2:1,2, it says, **And when the day of Pentecost had fully come, they were all** assembled together in one place, When suddenly. . . . Then it was all over but the shouting. That is the way God wants to move in our lives. You have waited and waited and waited, and you have had the horrible mess so long you feel like you can't stand it one more second. But you keep waiting on God and trusting in Him with a sweet and simple faith. Then when you least expect it and in a way that you could have *never* figured out, God moves *suddenly*! When you are looking at the front door, God will sneak in the back door. When you are looking out the window, He will come down through the chimney. *Suddenly*! When God moves in your life, things will begin to happen.

Stop Trying to Figure Out God

One of my favorite Scriptures is in Exodus 33 where God gave me some revelation on His glory. In verse 18, Moses said, show me Your glory. In verse 20 God said, **You can not see My face, for no man shall see Me and live.** Then in verse 21, He goes on and says: . . . Behold, there is a place beside Me, and you shall stand upon the rock, And while My glory passes by, I will put you in a cleft of the rock and cover you with My hand until I have passed by. Then I will take away My hand and you shall see My back; but My face shall not be seen.

I used to read that and wonder, "So what does that mean?" Then one day God showed me that we don't always, or even usually, see God coming, but we sure know when He has been there! In the meantime, we can stay hidden in the Rock, and that isn't a bad place to be! In other words, He said, "I'll hide you here in the rock till I pass by, and when I do, you won't see Me coming, but you'll know I've been there."

I don't know about you, but I have had that happen in my life so many times. Dave and I were waiting for a financial miracle in the ministry, then *all of a sudden* it happened! When you get to the point that you are done with your own works; you are done with trying to make it happen yourself, your way; then *suddenly*! *Suddenly* God will make it happen!

It gets to be an exciting way to live because every day you can get up without having to try to figure out what you are going to do. Instead you say, "God, I don't have any time for that. I have some living to do!"

It is also time for the Church to start living and to let go of the heavy burden it has been carrying around for so long. The Church needs to cast its cares on God and stop trying to figure out what He is doing.

Let Go of the Burden of Reasoning

The burden of reasoning is one of the greatest burdens that you can take on. You will know that you have taken it on when you find yourself asking questions like, "Well, how is God going to do it? What is He doing? When is He going to do it?"

Let's look again at Acts 1. In verse 4, He has just told them to wait for the promise of the Spirit. In verse 5, He tells them, **For John baptized with water, but not many days from now you shall be baptized with (placed in, introduced into) the Holy Spirit.** But they were still trying to figure things out. So in verse 6, when they were all assembled, they ask him, **Lord, is this the time when You will reestablish the kingdom and restore it to Israel?**

He says to them in verse 7: **It is not for you to become acquainted with and know what time brings [the things and events of time and** their definite periods] or fixed years and seasons (their critical niche in time), which the Father has appointed (fixed and reserved) by His own choice and authority and personal power.

In other words, God is saying, "No, no, no, no, no! I'm not going to tell you when. I'm not going to tell you next Thursday at two o'clock."

I'm not saying God never tells you when He is going to move because at certain times He does tell you. But *usually* God doesn't work that way. Usually, you don't have the slightest idea when the answer is going to come. When you think it is, it isn't! When you least expect it, *suddenly* it comes! Actually, we should be expecting, but sometimes we just get relaxed enough that God sneaks up on us and gives us a miracle.

Miracles Still Happen

Our younger son, Dan, who is now seventeen, has a really vivacious personality. He has always had a difficult time being quiet in school and obeying the rules, especially about talking. From the time he was in pre-kindergarten, I *knew* what I was going to hear when I went in for the teacher's report, "He just can't keep quiet." One teacher expressed it in a clever way when she said, "I think he has overly developed social skills."

In addition to talking too much, he was facing some other struggles like getting his work done, and it was beginning to affect his grades. At this point, we had done everything we knew to do. We had corrected. We had punished. We had talked. We had prayed. We had begged. We had pleaded. We had threatened. This had gone on for years and years. Now it was coming down to the wire, and his teachers were laying down some pretty strict rules he would have to abide by or else.

So we encouraged him to pray and believe God for a solution, and we continued to pray and believe God as well. By this time, I was telling God, "I can't do anything, God. I don't know what to do anymore. I'm all out of bright ideas. Either you are going to touch this kid and do something, or it isn't going to get done. I'm not driving myself nuts over this anymore because I really don't know what to do."

Then one day he came home from school and said, "We had a special prayer in school today, and the youth leader, Tom, got a word of knowledge for me. He said, 'Dan, I feel like I'm supposed to pray for you concerning some situations that you're having in school.' Then he had all the kids come over and lay their hands on me, and the power of God came on me in such a way that I got so hot Tom had to take his hand off of me. He couldn't even keep his hand on me anymore because I broke out in this sweat. Something happened to me. I don't know what it was, but something happened to me."

When he finished, I said, "Dan, what are you going to do?" And he simply said, "I'm going to be different." Then he got these big tears in his eyes and said, "Nobody is listening to me, but I'm telling you. I'm different. God touched me, and I'm different. There is nothing I can do about what I've done in the past. All I can do is just tell my teachers that I'm different, and they'll just have to wait and see."

So he told them the whole story and concluded by telling them that he was different now. When Dave went in the next time for the parent-teacher conference, *every* teacher gave him a glowing report. Now that is a miracle. He even got to go on a special trip that only a few out of around sixty kids were asked to go on because he had kept quiet and been good for that quarter.

All he was doing was waiting on God, then *suddenly* God moved. When you are waiting on God, He is going to do something for you. I can't tell you exactly how long it will take, but it will surely come. If we can ever get rid of the works of our flesh, it may even come sooner. I believe if I had been running around behind the scenes trying to fix this and figure that out, that it may have even taken longer because I wasn't really trusting God.

I'm not saying that you never do anything. If God gives you something to do, do it. But if He doesn't, don't. In my situation, I had done everything God had ever thought about giving me to do twenty-five times over. But, most probably, God never gave me much of it to do anyway. I was just doing it because I thought something needed to be done now, and I was going to see that it got done whether God was in it or not.

Learn to Wait Well

Sometimes we don't know how to wait, or we don't wait too well. Paul and Silas knew how to wait well. In Acts 16:22, the Scriptures tell us that a crowd attacked them and that the rulers tore off their clothes and commanded that they be beaten with rods and struck with many blows. Afterward, they were thrown into prison, and the jailer was charged to keep them safely.

So there they were sitting in this prison all beaten up with their clothes torn off of them. Verse 24 tells us that the jailer **having received [so strict a] charge, put them into the inner prison (the dungeon) and fastened their feet in** the stocks. He was going to make sure they didn't get out.

But then about midnight, God showed up. Wouldn't it have been nice if He had shown up around three o'clock in the afternoon? Why does He always wait until midnight—the darkest part of the night when everything is quiet?

Paul and Silas didn't seem to mind because verse 25 says, **But about midnight, as Paul and Silas were praying and singing hymns of praise to God. . . .** It sounds to me like they were waiting and saying to themselves, "Well, God, if you want to get us out of here, here we are. If not, I guess we'll stay, but either way we are going to be happy."

Verse 25 goes on to say:

> . . . and the [other] prisoners were
> listening to them, Suddenly there was
> a great earthquake, so that the very

foundations of the prison were
shaken . . . (VERSES 25,26).

You ought to draw a circle around all of the
"suddenly's" in your Bible because this is a
Word from God for you. Every time you find a
description in the Bible of people who were waiting on God in the midst of horrible circumstances, *suddenly* God broke through. Those
circumstances can't stand for one second before
the power of God. When God moves, your circumstances don't have a chance. But when *you*
start messing with your circumstances, you will
only increase them and make them worse. So let
God deal with them.

We talk so much about believing God, but
how many of us really, really, really know how to
believe God? First of all, the Bible says in
Hebrews 4:3 that *if* you are believing God, you
have entered His rest. How many people do you

know have really entered the rest of God? Maybe there will be a handful of people here and there, but there aren't many.

Those who have really believed do enter the rest of God. When you are in that place of waiting, you aren't trying to do it. And if you aren't trying to do it, you have time to have joy, and you will be able to wait well because you are resting in Him.

Waiting on God Brings Deliverance

When God shows up, not only do you get free, but those around you do too. Acts 16:26 says, Suddenly there was a great earthquake, so that the very foundations of the prisons were shaken; and at once all the doors were opened and everyone's shackles were unfastened.

I like that *suddenly* and *all at once* everybody got in on it. Do you understand that? God can flood the room and set everybody free. The doors flew open and everybody's shackles were loosed.

At one of our annual women's conferences, the Holy Ghost showed up in a uniquely special way and just flooded the room with His Spirit. People all over the room got touched and healed and delivered from something.

Now you don't have to be in some meeting to have the Holy Ghost minister to you. God touches me in powerful ways a whole lot more often in my private time with Him. You can have a good time between you and God any time you want to. You don't have to wait for some preacher to show up or somebody else who is anointed to show up. You just need to start waiting and spending time in the presence of God humbling yourself.

When you humble yourself, you cast all your care on God because He cares for you.

(1 Peter 5:6,7.) You give the whole mess to Him and say, "If you want me to stay this way until the trumpet blows, here I am. You love me just the way I am. If you want to change me, go for it." Paul and Silas humbled themselves before God. They gave the whole mess to Him, and He changed their circumstances. He delivered them and everybody else.

When you are really walking by faith, there is joy because even though you don't know what God is going to do or when He is going to do it or how He is going to do it, you are excited because you know He is *going* to do it.

Waiting Brings Salvation

Maybe there is somebody in your life who isn't born again or isn't serving God, and you need God to suddenly show up in their life? Well, get ready. You are about to be encouraged. The same Paul who was praising and worshiping God in the midnight hour used to be called Saul and went around killing Christians. But God moved suddenly one day.

In Acts 22:4–10, he describes himself this way:

> I harassed (troubled, molested, and persecuted) this Way [of the Lord] to the death, putting in chains and committing to prison both men and women, As the high priest and whole council of elders (Sanhedrin) can testify; for from them indeed I received letters with which I was on my way to the brethren in Damascus in order to take also those [believers] who were

there, and bring them in chains to Jerusalem that they might be punished.

But as I was on my journey and approached Damascus, about noon a great blaze of light flashed suddenly from heaven and shone about me. And I fell to the ground and heard a voice saying to me, Saul, Saul, why do you persecute Me [harass and trouble and molest Me]?

And I replied, Who are You, Lord? And He said to me, I am Jesus the Nazarene, Whom you are persecuting. Now the men who were with me saw the light, but they did not hear [the sound of the uttered words of] the voice of the One Who was speaking to me [so that they could not understand it]. And I asked, What shall I do, Lord?

When God gets right in the middle of some-body's life, they change their tune. Now he is saying, **What shall I do, Lord?**

If there is someone who is unsaved in your life, you need to stop trying to save them. You need to stop playing the Holy Ghost, and you need to stop aggravating them. All you need to do is to say, "God, get 'em," then wait on Him to move.

One day they will just be going about their old sinful life doing what they normally do—to the bar, getting drunk, smoking pot or looking for a one-night stand—when suddenly, as with Paul, God will move in their life.

Do you know why it has to work this way? Because if it doesn't, God won't get the glory. And one thing that God isn't going to let you touch is His glory. Who knows what kinds of miracles you would see in your life if you could ever get your hands off of trying to do things in the flesh yourself.

We are always trying to mold ourselves, fix ourselves, shape ourselves and change ourselves. Just get your hands off of trying to change yourself and say, "God, if you can't do it, it doesn't need to get done." Then you wait. How long will you have to wait? That is the part I can't tell you because that is between you and God.

Waiting Takes Faith

Beginning in Mark 5:25 is the story of the woman with an issue of blood. She didn't have this flow of blood for ten minutes. No, she had been sick with this flow of blood for twelve years. Can you imagine that? For twelve, long years, this woman had been putting up with this mess.

The Scriptures put it this way in verse 26:

And who had endured much suffering under [the hands of] many physicians

and had spent all that she had, and
was no better but instead grew worse.

It goes on to say she had heard the reports
concerning Jesus, and had come up behind Him
in the throng and touched His garment. This
woman had not lost hope, and she had not given
up faith. If she would have been over in some
depressed, hopeless, despondent state, she would
have never gone out and pressed through that
crowd to touch Jesus. She had lived with the
issue of blood twelve years, but she was not
without hope. One of the biggest problems
people face is that they become hopeless.

Verses 28 and 29 say:

For she kept saying, If I only touch His
garments, I shall be restored to health.
And immediately her flow of blood
was dried up at the source, and

[suddenly] she felt in her body that
she was healed of her [distressing]
ailment.

And Jesus, recognizing in Himself
that the power proceeding from Him
had gone forth, turned around
immediately in the crowd and said,
Who touched My clothes?

When you get into that place of patiently
waiting on God, your faith will touch the throne,
and it will draw power to you like you have never
seen before. When that power comes, *suddenly*
the circumstances are going to have to bow their
knee. The woman with the issue of blood knew
this. That is why Jesus told her, her faith in Him,
not her circumstances, had made her whole.

We worship our circumstances far too
much. We pay far too much attention to our circumstances and give too little attention to the

name of Jesus. Every knee has to bow to that name. Every human knee, every demonic knee, every knee in heaven, on the earth and under the earth has to bow to the name of Jesus.

Real Faith Will Keep You Going

You say, "When?" We already read in Acts 1 that *when* isn't our business. Of course, when *suddenly* those things we have been waiting for manifest, it is wonderful and glorious. But even when you enter that place of waiting patiently, there is a sweet peace and a joy that comes from already enjoying spiritually what you know is eventually going to come in the natural.

I remember the day I was baptized in the Holy Spirit. I will never forget it. I guess most people who have been filled with the Holy Spirit never forget the day God touched them. At that time, my life was one big, longstanding mess even though I was a Christian and loved God. I went to church all the time and did everything I knew to do but was getting none the better.

I was like the lady with an issue of blood, but in my case it wasn't an issue of blood. It was a bloody mess of a different kind. I was a mess. My life was a mess, and I couldn't seem to change. I didn't have any power—I didn't have any power to be a witness. I was out doing door-to-door witnessing at the time, but I didn't have any power to be a witness. I knew all about the *doing* part, but I didn't know about the *being* part.

I was on my way to work one morning when I said to God, "I just give up. I can't go on like this anymore. You have to do something!" I didn't even know what I wanted Him to do because I thought I had already done it all. I didn't know God could do something that I couldn't do. I really got discouraged. I had done everything I knew to do, but it still wasn't working.

Why does God let us get to that point? Because He wants us to run out of ourselves so that we know we can't do it. But in order to see your situation change, you have to make the transition from "I can't" to "God can."

You may have tried everything and decided that nothing was going to work, then grown depressed and despondent in the process. You may have developed a bad attitude along the way and begun to crab and complain and make everybody, including yourself, miserable because you had done everything *you* could think of to do, and still it didn't look to you as though God was working.

Then you began to murmur at God saying, "I've done this, and I've done that. Now where are *You*?" You started sounding as though you deserve some big reward for all you put yourself through. But the reality is that He never asked you to do all that you did in the first place. They were all your ideas.

Sure He gave Abraham a promise. He said, "I will come around at the right season, your wife will conceive and you will have a child" (author's paraphrase). And Abraham believed God, but when God wasn't working on his timetable, it didn't take him and his wife too long to come up with a way to make sure this would come to pass. As a matter of fact, it only took them one chapter.

God made the promise to them in Genesis 15, and by Genesis 16, they were already impatient and upset. Sarah said, "I know what we will do." One of those little creative light bulbs went on in her head, and it wasn't long after that Ishmael was born. But Ishmael wasn't the one God had promised.

My situation wasn't much different. There I was driving around in my car telling God I couldn't go on like this anymore and that He needed to do something. It was then that God spoke to me in a loud, audible voice. There is no reason for me to tell you what He said because it only made sense to me, but I knew it was God, and I knew what He meant.

When He finished, I entered into a peace. I didn't have any idea what He was going to do, but at that point, I didn't care. I wasn't trying to figure it out, and it didn't make any difference to me if He did it today, tomorrow, next week or next year because I already had it in me.

The Bible says that faith, real faith, is the thing that keeps you going until the manifestation comes. When you have it inside of you, it is just like being pregnant. You don't wait until you have a baby to believe that you are going to have a baby. You don't wait until the day of the birth to get excited about the baby. You are excited from the minute the doctor says, "You are going to have a baby."

You are running around telling everybody, "I'm going to have a baby. I'm going to have a baby. I'm going to have a baby." How do you know you are going to have a baby? You don't look pregnant to other people. Well, you just are. Then you go about making plans and making a provision. You are happy and excited. Then, at the right time, you have a baby.

In my case, however, I didn't know what God was going to do, but I knew that I knew He was going to do something. I wouldn't have cared right then if it had taken ten years. I got my hair done that night after work and was driving down the highway on my way home. When I got to the exit ramp, I turned off the highway and was driving up the ramp when I said, "God, I don't care what You do or when You do it, but I know You are going to move and do something."

At the end of the ramp as I was waiting to turn onto another road, the power of the Holy Ghost hit me *suddenly*, and I was baptized in the Holy Spirit. And since that day I have never been the same. God moved *suddenly* in my life, but it was only after I had waited.

Let God Move in Your Life

You may need to apply what you have read here to your situation. If you do, God will touch you. But you must let Him. Wait patiently and expectantly, and at the right time God will move in your life *suddenly*!

ENDNOTES

1. James Strong, "Hebrew and Chaldee Dictionary" in *Strong's Exhaustive Concordance of the Bible* (Nashville: Abingdon, 1890), 51, #3327.

2. Andrew Murray, *The Promise of the Bible* (Grand Rapids: Zondervan Corporation, 1990).

ABOUT THE AUTHOR

JOYCE MEYER is one of the world's leading practical Bible teacher. A #1 *New York Times* bestselling author, she has written more than seventy inspirational books, including *Look Great, Feel Great*, the entire Battlefield of the Mind family of books, and many others. She has also released thousands of audio teachings as well as a complete video library. Joyce's *Enjoying Everyday Life*® radio and television programs are broadcast around the world, and she travels extensively conducting conferences. Joyce and her husband, Dave, are the parents of four grown children and make their home in St. Louis, Missouri.

To contact the author write:

Joyce Meyer Ministries
P. O. Box 655
Fenton, Missouri 63026
or call: (636) 349-0303

Internet Address: www.joycemeyer.org

Please include your testimony or help received from this book when you write. Your prayer requests are welcome.

To contact the author
in Canada, please write:
Joyce Meyer Ministries Canada, Inc.
Lambeth Box 1300
London, ON N6P 1T5
or call: (636) 349-0303

In Australia, please write:
Joyce Meyer Ministries-Australia
Locked Bag 77
Mansfield Delivery Centre
Queensland 4122
or call: (07) 3349 1200

In England, please write:
Joyce Meyer Ministries
P. O. Box 1549
Windsor
SL4 1GT

Or call: (0) 1753 831102

OTHER BOOKS BY JOYCE MEYER

Battlefield of the Mind *

Battlefield of the Mind Devotional

Approval Addiction

Ending Your Day Right

In Pursuit of Peace

The Secret Power of Speaking God's Word

Seven Things That Steal Your Joy

Starting Your Day Right

Beauty for Ashes Revised Edition

How to Hear from God *

Knowing God Intimately

The Power of Forgiveness

The Power of Determination

The Power of Being Positive

The Secrets of Spiritual Power

The Battle Belongs to the Lord

The Secrets to Exceptional Living

Eight Ways to Keep the Devil Under Your Feet

Teenagers Are People Too!

Filled with the Spirit

Celebration of Simplicity

* Study Guide available for this title

Expect a Move of God in Your Life . . . Suddenly!

*Enjoying Where You Are on the Way to
Where You Are Going*

The Most Important Decision You Will Ever Make

When, God, When?

Why, God, Why?

The Word, the Name, the Blood

Tell Them I Love Them

Peace

The Root of Rejection

If Not for the Grace of God *

JOYCE MEYER SPANISH TITLES

*Las Siete Cosas Que Te Roban el Gozo
(Seven Things That Steal Your Joy)*

*Empezando Tu Día Bien
(Starting Your Day Right)*

BOOKS BY DAVE MEYER

Life Lines